AF492775

BETHINK YOURSELVES

LECTOR HOUSE PUBLIC DOMAIN WORKS

This book is a result of an effort made by Lector House towards making a contribution to the preservation and repair of original classic literature. The original text is in the public domain in the United States of America, and possibly other countries depending upon their specific copyright laws.

In an attempt to preserve, improve and recreate the original content, certain conventional norms with regard to typographical mistakes, hyphenations, punctuations and/or other related subject matters, have been corrected upon our consideration. However, few such imperfections might not have been rectified as they were inherited and preserved from the original content to maintain the authenticity and construct, relevant to the work. The work might contain a few prior copyright references as well as page references which have been retained, wherever considered relevant to the part of the construct. We believe that this work holds historical, cultural and/or intellectual importance in the literary works community, therefore despite the oddities, we accounted the work for print as a part of our continuing effort towards preservation of literary work and our contribution towards the development of the society as a whole, driven by our beliefs.

We are grateful to our readers for putting their faith in us and accepting our imperfections with regard to preservation of the historical content. We shall strive hard to meet up to the expectations to improve further to provide an enriching reading experience.

Though, we conduct extensive research in ascertaining the status of copyright before redeveloping a version of the content, in rare cases, a classic work might be incorrectly marked as not-in-copyright. In such cases, if you are the copyright holder, then kindly contact us or write to us, and we shall get back to you with an immediate course of action.

HAPPY READING!

BETHINK YOURSELVES

LEO TOLSTOY,
AYLMER MAUDE

ISBN: 978-93-5614-019-6

Published: 1904

© 2022
LECTOR HOUSE LLP

LECTOR HOUSE

LECTOR HOUSE LLP
E-MAIL: lectorpublishing@gmail.com

BETHINK YOURSELVES

(CONCERNING
THE RUSSO-JAPANESE WAR)

BY

LEO TOLSTOY

**TRANSLATED BY
AYLMER MAUDE**

"This is your hour, and the power of darkness." Luke xxii.53

1904

CONTENTS

BETHINK YOURSELVES

CHAPTER I

Your iniquities have separated you from your God; your sins have hidden his face from you, so that he will not hear. For your hands are stained with blood, your fingers with guilt. Your lips have spoken lies, and your tongue mutters wicked things. No one calls for justice; no one pleads his case with integrity. They rely on empty arguments and speak lies; they conceive trouble and give birth to evil… Their deeds are evil deeds, and acts of violence are in their hands. Their feet rush into sin; they are swift to shed innocent blood. Their thoughts are evil thoughts; ruin and destruction mark their ways. The way of peace they do not know; there is no justice in their paths. They have turned them into crooked roads; no one who walks in them will know peace. So justice is far from us, and righteousness does not reach us. We look for light, but all is darkness; for brightness, but we walk in deep shadows. Like the blind we grope along the wall, feeling our way like men without eyes. At midday we stumble as if it were twilight; among the strong, we are like the dead. We all growl like bears; we moan mournfully like doves. We look for justice, but find none; we look for deliverance, but it is far away.

Isaiah lix:2-11.

War is held in greater esteem than ever. A skilled proficient in this business, that murderer of genius, von Moltke, once replied to some Peace delegates in the following terrible words:

"War is sacred; it is instituted by God; it is one of the divine laws of the world; it upholds in men all the great and noble sentiments: honor, self-sacrifice, virtue, and courage. It is War alone that saves men from falling into the grossest materialism."

To assemble four hundred thousand men in herds; to march night and day without rest, with no time to think, read, or study, without being of the least use to anybody; wallowing in filth; sleeping in the mud; living like animals in continual stupefaction; sacking towns; burning villages; ruining the whole population, and then meeting similar masses of human flesh and falling upon them; shedding rivers of blood; strewing the fields with mangled bodies mixed with mud and blood; losing arms and legs and having brains blown out for no benefit to anyone; dying somewhere on a field while your old parents, wife, and children are perishing of hunger – that is called saving men from falling into the grossest materialism!

Guy de Maupassant.

We will content ourselves with reminding you that the different states of Europe have accumulated a debt of a hundred and thirty billion francs (about a hundred and ten within the last century), and that this colossal debt has arisen almost exclusively from the expenses of war; that in times of peace they maintain standing armies of four million men, which they can increase to ten million in times of war;[1] that two-thirds of their budgets are absorbed by interest on these debts and by the maintenance of land and sea forces.

Gustave de Molinari.

Again there is war! Again there is needless and quite unnecessary suffering, together with fraud and a general stupefaction and brutalization of men.

These men are separated from each other by thousands of miles – Buddhists whose law forbids the killing not only of men but even of animals, and Christians professing a law of brotherhood and love. Hundreds of thousands of such men seek one another out on land and sea like wild beasts to kill, torture, and mutilate one another in the cruelest possible way. Can this really be happening, or is it merely a dream? Something impossible and unbelievable is taking place, and one longs to believe that it is a dream and to awaken from it.

But it is no dream. It is a dreadful reality.

It is understandable that a poor, uneducated Japanese may have been torn from his field and taught that Buddhism consists not in having compassion for all that lives, but in offering sacrifices to idols. And it is understandable that a similar poor illiterate fellow from the neighborhood of Túla or Nízhni-Nóvgorod may have been taught that Christianity consists in bowing before icons of Christ, the Mother of God, and the Saints. It is understandable that these unfortunate men, taught by centuries of violence and deceit to regard the greatest crime in the world – the murder of their fellow men – as a noble deed, could commit these dreadful crimes without regarding themselves as guilty. But how can so-called enlightened men support war, preach it, participate in it, and, worst of all, without being exposed to its dangers themselves, incite their unfortunate, defrauded brothers to take part in it? These so-called enlightened men cannot help knowing, I do not say

---

[1] Now, in 1936, these figures have enormously increased and continue to expand.–A.M.

the Christian law (if they recognize themselves to be Christians), but all that has been and is being written and said about the cruelty, futility, and senselessness of war. They are regarded as enlightened just because they know all this. Most of them have themselves written and spoken about it. Not to mention the Hague Conference, which evoked universal praise, and all the books, pamphlets, newspaper articles, and speeches concerning the possibility of solving international misunderstandings by international courts. No enlightened man can help knowing that universal competition in the armaments of different states must inevitably result in endless wars and general bankruptcy, or in both of these together. They cannot help knowing that besides the insensate and useless expenditure of billions of rubles on preparations for war, millions of the most energetic and vigorous men perish in wars at the most productive time of their lives. (Fourteen million men have so perished during the past century.) Enlightened men cannot but know that the grounds of a war are never worth a single human life or a hundredth part of what is spent on it. (In fighting for the emancipation of the Negroes, much more was spent than would have bought all the slaves in the Southern States.)

Above all, everyone knows and cannot but know that wars evoke the lowest animal passions and deprave and brutalize men. Everyone knows how unconvincing the arguments in favor of war are (such as those brought forward by de Maistre,[2] von Moltke, and others). They are all based on the sophistry that it is possible to find a useful side in every human calamity, or on the quite arbitrary assertion that wars must always exist because they have always existed – as if the evil actions of men can be justified by the advantages they bring or by the fact that they have long been committed. Every so-called enlightened man knows all this. But suddenly a war begins and it is all instantly forgotten, and the very men who only yesterday were proving the cruelty, futility, and senselessness of wars, now think, speak, and write only of how to kill as many men as possible, of how to ruin and destroy as much of the produce of human labor as possible, and how to inflame the passion of hatred to the utmost in those peaceful, harmless, industrious men who by their labor feed, clothe, and maintain the pseudo-enlightened men who force them to commit these dreadful deeds, contrary to their consciences, welfare, and faith.

---

[2] Joseph de Maistre was an ardent Roman Catholic who acted as Sardinian ambassador at Petersburg from 1803 to 1817.–A.M.

CHAPTER II

And Micromegas said:

"O intelligent atoms in whom the Eternal Being has been pleased to manifest his dexterity and his might, the joys you taste on your globe are doubtless very pure, for as you are so immaterial and seem to be all spirit, your lives must be passed in Love and in Thought. That indeed is the true life of spirits. Nowhere yet have I found real happiness, but that you have it here I cannot doubt."

At these words all the philosophers shook their heads and one of them, more frank than the rest, candidly admitted that apart from a small number of people who were held in little esteem, the rest of the inhabitants of the world were a crowd of madmen, miscreants, and unfortunates. "If evil is a property of matter," he said, "we have more matter than is necessary for the doing of much evil, and too much spirit if evil be a property of the spirit. Do you realize, for instance, that at this moment there are a hundred thousand madmen of our species wearing hats, killing or being killed by a hundred thousand other animals wearing turbans, and that over almost the whole face of the earth this has been the custom from time immemorial?"

The Sirian shuddered and asked what could be the ground for these horrible quarrels between such puny beasts.

"The matter at issue," replied the philosopher, "is some mudheap as large as your heel. It is not that any single man of all these millions who slaughter each other claims one straw on the mudheap. The point is: shall the mud-heap belong to a certain man called the Sultan, or to another called Caesar? I know not why. Neither of them has ever seen or will ever see the little bit of land in dispute, and barely one of these animals which slaughter each other has ever seen the animal for which he is slaughtered."

"Wretches!" cried the Sirian indignantly. "Such a riot of mad fury is inconceivable! I am tempted to take three steps and with three blows of my foot crush out of existence this ant-hill of absurd cut-throats."

"Do not trouble yourself," answered the philosopher. "They

wreak their own ruin. Know that after ten years not a hundredth part of these miscreants is ever left. Know that even when they have not drawn the sword, hunger, exhaustion, or debauchery carries them nearly all off. Besides, it is not they who should be punished, but the stay-at-home barbarians who, after a good meal, order from their remote closets the massacre of a million men, and then have solemn prayers of gratitude for the event offered up to God."

Voltaire, Micromegas, Ch. vii.

The folly of modern wars is excused on grounds of dynastic interests, nationality, European equilibrium, and honor. This last is perhaps the most extravagant excuse of all, for there is not a nation in the world that has not polluted itself by all sorts of crimes and shameful actions, nor is there one that has not experienced every possible humiliation. If indeed there still exists a sense of honor among nations, it is strange to support it by making war – that is, by committing all the crimes by which a private person dishonors himself: arson, rape, outrage, murder…

Anatole France.

The savage instinct of murder-in-war has very deep roots in the human brain, because it has been carefully encouraged and cultivated for thousands of years. One likes to hope that a humanity superior to ours will succeed in correcting this original vice, but what will it then think of this civilization calling itself refined and of which we are so proud? Even now, at one and the same time, we think of ancient Mexico and of its cannibalism as pious, warlike, and bestial.

Charles Letourneau.

Sometimes one ruler attacks another out of fear in order that the latter should not fall upon him. Sometimes war is begun because the foe is too strong, and sometimes because he is too weak. Sometimes our neighbors desire our possessions, or they possess what we want. Then begins war, which lasts until they seize what they may require or surrender the possession that is demanded by us.

Jonathan Swift.

Something incomprehensible and impossible in its cruelty, falsehood, and stupidity is taking place. The Russian Tsar, the very man who summoned all the nations to peace,[3] publicly announces that, despite his efforts to maintain the

---

[3] This refers to the Hague Conference of 1899, organized at the instance of Nicholas II,

peace so dear to his heart (efforts expressed by the seizure of other peoples' lands, and the strengthening of the army for the defense of these stolen lands), in consequence of attacks by the Japanese, he is compelled to order the same to be done to them as they have begun doing to the Russians, that is, that they should be killed. In announcing this call to murder he mentions God, evoking a Divine blessing on the most dreadful crime in the world. The Japanese Emperor has proclaimed the same thing in regard to the Russians.

Learned jurists, Messieurs Muravev and Martens, are assiduous in demonstrating that, because other peoples' lands have been seized, there is no contradiction at all between the former general call to universal peace and the present incitement to war. Diplomats publish and send out circulars in the refined French language, proving circumstantially and diligently (though they know that no one believes them) that after all its efforts to establish peaceful relations (in reality after all its efforts to deceive other countries) the Russian government has been compelled to have recourse to the only means for a rational solution of the question: the murder of men. And the Japanese diplomats write the same thing. Learned men for their part, comparing the present with the past and deducing profound conclusions from these comparisons, argue interminably about the laws of the movements of nations, about the relation of the yellow to the white race, and about Buddhism and Christianity. On the basis of these deductions and reflections they justify the slaughter of the yellow race by Christians. And in the same way the Japanese learned men and philosophers justify the slaughter of the white race. Journalists, with unconcealed joy, trying to outdo one another and not stopping at any falsehood however impudent and transparent, prove in various ways that the Russians alone are right and strong and good in every respect, that all the Japanese are wrong and weak and bad in every respect, and that all those who are inimical or who may become inimical towards the Russians (the English and the Americans) are bad too. And the Japanese and their supporters prove just the same regarding the Russians.

Quite apart from the military people whose profession it is to prepare for murder, crowds of supposedly enlightened people – professors, social reformers, students, gentry, and merchants – of their own accord express the most bitter and contemptuous feelings towards the Japanese, the English, and the Americans, towards whom only yesterday they were well disposed or indifferent. And of their own accord they express most abject and servile feelings towards the Tsar (to whom they are completely indifferent, to say the least), assuring him of their unbounded love and readiness to sacrifice their lives for him.

And that unfortunate and entangled young man, acknowledged as ruler of a hundred and thirty million people, continually deceived and obliged to contradict himself, believes all this, and thanks and blesses for slaughter the troops he calls his, in defense of lands he has even less right to call his. They all present hideous icons to one another (in which no enlightened people now believe and which even uneducated peasants are beginning to abandon) and they all bow to the ground before these icons, kiss them, and pronounce pompous and false speeches which

---

and aiming at an agreement not to increase the armed forces that then existed.–A.M.

nobody believes.

Wealthy people contribute insignificant portions of their immorally acquired riches to this cause of murder, or to the organization of assistance in the work of murder, while the poor, from whom the government annually collects two billion rubles, deem it necessary to do likewise, offering their mites also. The government incites and encourages crowds of idlers who walk about the streets with the Tsar's portrait, singing and shouting hurrah and committing all kinds of excesses under pretext of patriotism. All over Russia, from the capital to the remotest village, the priests in the churches, calling themselves Christians, appeal to the God who enjoined love of one's enemies, the God of love, for help in the devil's work: the slaughter of men.

And stupefied by prayers, sermons, exhortations, processions, pictures, and newspapers, the cannon-fodder – hundreds of thousands of men dressed alike and carrying various lethal weapons – leave their parents, wives, and children. With agony at heart and a show of bravado, they go where, at the risk of their own lives, they will commit the most dreadful action: killing men whom they do not know and who have done them no harm. And in their wake go doctors and nurses who, for some reason, suppose that they cannot serve the simple, peaceful, suffering people at home, but can serve only those who are engaged in slaughtering one another. Those who remain behind rejoice at the news of the murder of men, and when they learn that a great many Japanese have been killed they thank someone whom they call God.

And not only is all this considered a manifestation of elevated feeling, but those who refrain from such manifestations and attempt to bring people to reason are considered traitors and enemies to their nation, and are in danger of being abused and beaten by a brutalized crowd that possesses no other weapon but brute force in defense of its insanity and cruelty.

CHAPTER III

War organizes a body of men who lose the feelings of the citizen in the soldier; whose habits detach them from the community; whose ruling passion is devotion to a chief; who are inured in camp to despotic sway; who are accustomed to accomplish their ends by force and to sport with the rights and happiness of their fellow beings; who delight in tumult, adventure, and peril, and turn with disgust and scorn from the quiet labors of peace... It (war) tends to multiply and perpetuate itself endlessly. The successful nation, flushed by victory, pants for new laurels, while the humbled nation, irritated by defeat, is impatient to redeem its honor and repair its losses...

Instead of awakening pity, the slaughter of thousands of fellow beings flushes them with delirious joy, illuminates the city, and dissolves the whole country in revelry and riot. Thus the heart of man is hardened and his worst passions are nourished. He renounces the bonds and sympathies of humanity.

Channing.

The age for military service has arrived, and every young man has to submit to the arbitrary orders of some rascal or ignoramus. He must believe that nobility and greatness consist in renouncing his own will and becoming the tool of another's will, in slashing and in getting himself slashed, in suffering from hunger, thirst, rain, and cold; in being mutilated without knowing why and without any other reward than a glass of brandy on the day of battle and the promise of something impalpable and fictitious: immortality after death, and glory given or refused by the pen of some journalist in his warm room.

A gun is fired. He falls wounded. His comrades finish him off by trampling over him. He is buried half alive and then he may enjoy immortality. The one for whom he had given his happiness, his sufferings, and his very life, never knew him. And years later someone comes to collect his whitened bones, out of which they make paint and English blacking for cleaning his General's boots.

Alphonse Karr.

They take a man in the bloom of his youth, they put a gun

into his hands, a knapsack on his back, and a cockaded hat on his head, and then they say to him: "My brother-ruler of so-and-so has treated me badly. You must attack his subjects. I have informed them that on such and such a date you will present yourselves at the frontier to slaughter them... Perhaps at first you will think that our enemies are men, but they are not men – they are Prussians or Frenchmen. You will distinguish them from the human race by the color of their uniforms. Try to do your duty well, for I am looking on. If you gain the victory, they will bring you to the windows of my palace when you return. I will come down in full uniform and say, 'Soldiers, I am satisfied!' Should you remain on the battlefield (which may easily happen), I will communicate the news of your death to your family that they may mourn for you and inherit your share of things. If you lose an arm or a leg I will pay you what they are worth. But I will dismiss you if you remain alive and are no longer fit to carry your knapsack, and you can go and die where you like. That will no longer concern me."

Claude Tillier.

But I learned discipline, namely, that the corporal is always right when he addresses a private, the sergeant when he addresses a corporal, the sub-lieutenant when he addresses a sergeant-major, and so on up to the Field-Marshal – even should they say that twice two is five!

It is at first difficult to grasp this, but there is something that will help you to understand it. It is a notice stuck up in the barracks, and which is read to you from time to time in order to clear your ideas. This notice sets out all that a soldier may wish to do – to return to his village, to refuse to serve, to disobey his commander, and so on – and for all this the penalty is mentioned: capital punishment, or five years' penal servitude.

Erckmann-Chatrian.

I have bought a Negro, and he is mine. He works like a horse. I feed him badly, I clothe him similarly, and he is beaten when he disobeys. Is there anything surprising in that? Do we treat our soldiers any better? Are they not deprived of liberty like this Negro? The only difference is that the soldier costs much less. A good Negro is now worth at least five hundred écus, but a good soldier is hardly worth fifty. Neither the one nor the other may quit the place where he is confined. Both are beaten for the slightest fault. Their salaries are about the same. But the Negro has this advantage over the soldier: he does not risk his life but passes it with his wife and children.

Questions sur l'Encyclopédie, par des amateurs, Art. Esclavage.

It is as if neither Voltaire, nor Montaigne, nor Pascal, nor Swift, nor Kant, nor Spinoza had ever existed, nor the hundreds of other writers who have very forcibly exposed the madness and futility of war, and described its cruelty, immorality, and savagery. Above all, it is as if Jesus and his teaching of human brotherhood and love of God and man had never existed.

Recalling all this and looking around on what is happening now, one experiences horror less at the abominations of war than at that most horrible of all horrors, the consciousness of the impotence of human reason. Reason, which alone distinguishes man from the brutes and constitutes his true dignity, is now regarded as an unnecessary, useless, and even pernicious attribute that simply impedes action, like a bridle dangling from a horse's head, merely entangling his legs and irritating him.

It is understandable that a pagan, a Greek, a Roman, or even a medieval Christian ignorant of the Gospel and blindly believing all the prescriptions of the Church, might fight, and while fighting pride himself on his military calling. But how can a believing Christian, or even a skeptic involuntarily permeated by the Christian ideals of human brotherhood and love that have inspired the works of the philosophers, moralists, and artists of our time – how can such a man take a gun or stand by a cannon and aim at a crowd of his fellow men, desiring to kill as many of them as possible?

The Assyrians, Romans, or Greeks might be convinced that they not only acted according to their conscience but even performed a good action when fighting. But we are Christians whether we wish it or not, and the general spirit of Christianity (however it may have been distorted) has lifted us to a higher plane of reason, whence we cannot but feel with our whole being not only the senselessness and cruelty of war but also its complete contrast to all that we regard as good and right. And so we cannot quietly do as they did with assurance and firmness. We cannot do it without a consciousness of our criminality, without the desperate feeling of a murderer who, having begun to kill his victim and aware in the depths of his soul of his guilt, tries to stupefy or infuriate himself in order to be able to complete his dreadful deed. All the unnatural, feverish, hotheaded, insane excitement that has now seized the idle upper ranks of Russian society is merely a symptom of their consciousness of the criminality of what is being done. All these swaggering mendacious speeches about devotion to, and worship of, the monarch; all this readiness to sacrifice their lives (they should say other people's lives); all these promises to defend with their breasts land that does not belong to them; all these senseless blessings of one another with various banners and monstrous icons; all these Te Deums; all this preparation of blankets and bandages; all these detachments of nurses; all these contributions to the fleet and to the Red Cross presented to the government – whose direct duty it is, having declared war (and being able to collect as much money as it requires from the people), to organize the necessary fleet and necessary means for attending the wounded – all these pompous, senseless, and blasphemous Slavonic prayers, the utterance of which the papers report as important news in various towns; all these processions, calls for the national anthem, and shouts of hurrah; all this desperate newspaper mendacity, which has no fear of exposure because it is so general; all this stupefaction and brutalization in which Russian society is now plunged, and which is transmitted by degrees to the masses – all this is merely a symptom of the consciousness of guilt in the dreadful thing that is being done.

Spontaneous feeling tells men that what they are doing is wrong, but as a murderer who has begun to assassinate his victim cannot stop, so the fact of the deadly work having been begun seems to Russian people an unanswerable reason in its favor. War has begun, and so it must go on. So it seems to simple, benighted, unlearned men under the influence of the petty passions and stupefaction to which they have been subjected. And in the same way the most learned men of our time demonstrate that man has no free will, and that therefore, even if he understands that the thing he has begun is evil, he cannot stop doing it.

And so, dazed and brutalized, men continue the dreadful work.

CHAPTER IV

It is amazing to what an extent the most insignificant disagreement can become a sacred war, thanks to diplomacy and the newspapers. When England and France declared war on Russia in 1853 it came about from such insignificant reasons that a long search among the diplomatic archives is necessary to discover it... The death of five hundred thousand good men and the expenditure of from five to six billion francs were the consequences of that strange misunderstanding.

Motives existed. But they were such as were not acknowledged. Napoleon the Third wished by an alliance with England and a successful war to consolidate his power, which was of criminal origin. The Russians hoped to obtain possession of Constantinople. The English wished to assure the triumph of their commerce, and to hinder Russian influence in the East. In one shape or another it is always the spirit of conquest or of violence.

Charles Richet.

Can anything be more stupid than that a man has the right to kill me because he lives on the other side of a river and his ruler has a quarrel with mine, though I have not quarreled with him?

Pascal.

The inhabitants of the planet Earth are still in a ridiculous state of unintelligence and stupidity. Every day in the newspapers of the civilized countries, we read a discussion of the diplomatic relations of the chiefs of states aiming at an alliance against a supposed enemy and preparations for war. These nations allow their leaders to dispose of them like cattle led to the slaughter, as though never suspecting that the life of each man is his personal property.

The inhabitants of this singular planet have been reared in the conviction that there are nations, frontiers, and standards. They have such a feeble sense of humanity that that feeling is completely effaced by the sense of the Fatherland... It is true that this situation would change if those who think could come to an agreement, for individually no one desires war... But there exist these political combinations, which furnish livelihood for a legion of parasites.

Flammarion.

When we study, not superficially but fundamentally, the various activities of mankind, we cannot avoid sad reflection on how many lives are expended for the perpetuation of the power of evil on earth, and how this evil is promoted most of all by permanent armies.

Our astonishment and feeling of sadness increase when we consider that this is all unnecessary, and that this evil complacently accepted by the immense majority of men comes about merely through their stupidity in allowing a comparatively small number of agile and perverted people to exploit them.

Patrice Larroque.

Ask a soldier – a private, a corporal, or a noncommissioned officer, who has abandoned his old parents, his wife and children – why he is preparing to kill men he does not know, and he will at first be surprised at your question. He is a soldier, has taken the oath, and must fulfill the orders of his commanders. If you tell him that war – the slaughter of men – does not conform to the command, "Thou shalt not kill," he will say, "But what if our people are attacked?" and, "For the Tsar and the Orthodox Faith!" (In answer to my question, one of them said, "But what if he attacks what is sacred?" "What do you mean?" I asked. "Why," said he, "the flag.") If you try to explain to such a soldier that God's command is more important than the flag, or more important than anything in the world, he will become silent or will get angry and report you to the authorities.

Ask an officer or a general why he goes to the war. He will tell you that he is a military man, and that military men are indispensable for the defense of the Fatherland. It does not trouble him that murder is not in agreement with the spirit of the Christian law, because he either does not believe in that law or, if he does, he does not believe in that law itself but in some explanation that has been given of it. Above all (like the soldier), he always asks a general question about the State or the Fatherland instead of the personal question regarding what he himself should do. "At the present time, when the Fatherland is in danger, one must act and not argue," he will say.

Ask the diplomats, who prepare wars by their deceptions, why they do it. They will tell you that the object of their activity is the establishment of peace among nations, and that this object is attained not by ideal, unrealizable theories, but by diplomatic activity and by being prepared for war. And just as military men ask a general question instead of a personal one affecting their own lives, so the diplomats will speak of the interests of Russia, of the perfidy of other Powers, or of the balance of power in Europe instead of about their own lives and activities.

Ask journalists why they incite men to war by their writings. They will say that, in general, wars are necessary and useful, especially the present one. They will confirm this by misty patriotic phrases, and (like the military men and the diplomats) they will talk about the general interests of the nation, the State, civilization, and the White Race, instead of saying why they themselves – particular individuals and living men – act in a certain way.

And all those who prepare for war will explain their participation in that work in just the same way. They will perhaps agree that it would be desirable to abolish war, but at present, they say, that is impossible. At present, as Russians and as men occupying certain positions – marshals of the gentry, members of local government, doctors, and workers in the Red Cross – they are called on to act and not to argue. "There is no time to argue and think about ourselves," they will say, "while there is a great common work to be done."

The Tsar, who is apparently responsible for the whole affair, will say the same. Like the soldier, he will be astonished at being asked whether or not war is now necessary. He does not even admit the idea that it might yet be stopped. He will say that he cannot fail to fulfill what is demanded of him by the whole nation, that – though he recognizes war to be a great evil and has used and is ready to use every possible means to abolish it – in the present case he could not help declaring war and cannot but go on with it. It is necessary for the welfare and glory of Russia.

Every one of these men recognizes the Christian law as binding on him – a law that forbids the killing of one's neighbor and demands that one should love and serve him. And yet, when asked why he permits himself to take part in war (that is, in violence, looting, and murder), every one of them will always answer that he does so for his Fatherland, his faith, his oath, his honor, civilization, or the future welfare of all mankind – in general, for something abstract and indefinite. Moreover, all these men are always so urgently occupied by preparation for war, its organization, or discussions about it that their leisure is taken up in resting from their labors. They have no time for discussions about their lives, and regard such discussions as idle.

CHAPTER V

The mind revolts at the inevitable catastrophe awaiting us, but it is necessary to prepare for it. For twenty years all the powers of knowledge have been exhausted in inventing engines of destruction, and soon a few cannon shots will suffice to destroy a whole army.

It is no longer as it was formerly, when a few thousand mercenary wretches were under arms. Whole nations are preparing to kill one another… And in order to fit them for murder, their hatred is excited by assurances that they themselves are hated. Kind-hearted men will believe this, and peaceful citizens, having received an absurd order to slay one another for God knows what ridiculous boundary incident or commercial colonial interests, will soon fling themselves at one another with the ferocity of wild beasts.

They will go to the slaughter like sheep, but with a knowledge of where they are going, that they are leaving their wives, and that their children will be hungry. But they will be so deceived and inebriated by false, bombastic words, that they will call on God to bless their bloody deeds. They will go with enthusiastic songs, cries of joy, and festive music, trampling down the harvest they have sown and burning towns they have built. They will go without indignation, humbly and submissively, despite the fact that the strength is theirs and that if they could only agree, they could establish common sense and fraternity in place of the savage frauds of diplomacy.

Edouard Rod.

An eyewitness relates what he saw when he stepped on to the deck of the Varyág during the present Russo-Japanese war. The sight was dreadful. Headless trunks, arms that had been torn off, and fragments of flesh were lying about in profusion, and everywhere there was blood, and a smell of blood which nauseated even those most accustomed to it. The conning tower had suffered most – a shell had exploded on it and had killed a young officer who was directing the sighting of the guns. All that was left of that unfortunate young man was a clenched hand holding an instrument. Two men who were with the captain were blown to pieces, and two others were severely wounded (both had to have their legs amputated, and then had to undergo a second amputation higher up). The captain escaped with a blow on the head from the splinter of a shell.

And this is not all. The wounded cannot be taken on board neutral ships because of the infection from gangrene and fever. Gangrene and suppurating wounds, together with hunger, fire, ruin, typhus, smallpox, and other infectious diseases, are also incidental to military glory. Such is war.

And yet Joseph de Maistre sang the praises of the beneficence of war: "When the human soul loses its resilience owing to effeminacy, when it becomes unbelieving and contracts those rotten vices which accompany the superfluities of civilization, it can only be re-established in blood."

M. de Vogue, the academician, says much the same thing, and so does M. Brunetiere. But the unfortunates of whom cannon-fodder is made have a right to disagree with this.

Unfortunately, however, they have not the courage of their convictions. Therein lies the whole evil. Accustomed from of old to allow themselves to be killed on account of questions they do not understand, they continue to let this be done, imagining all to be well.

That is why corpses are now lying beneath the water and are being devoured by crabs. When everything around them was being demolished by grapeshot, these unfortunates can hardly have consoled themselves by the thought that all this was being done for their good and to re-establish the souls of their contemporaries, which had lost their resilience from the superfluities of civilization. They had probably not read Joseph de Maistre.

I advise the wounded to read him between two dressings, and they will learn that war is as necessary as the executioner, because like him it is a manifestation of the justice of God. This great thought may serve them as consolation while the surgeons are sawing their bones!

Hardouin.

In the *Russian News* I read the opinion that Russia's advantage lies in her inexhaustible store of human material. For children whose father is killed, for a wife whose husband is killed, for a mother whose son is killed – this material is quickly exhausted.

From a private letter from a Russian mother, March 1904

You ask whether war is *still* necessary between civilized nations.

I reply that not only is it no longer necessary, but that it never has been necessary. It has always violated the historical development of humanity, infringed human rights, and hindered progress.

If some of the consequences of war have been advantageous to civilization in general, its harmful consequences have been much greater. We are misled because only a part of these harmful consequences is immediately apparent. The greater part and the most important we do not notice. So we must not accept the word "still." Its acceptance gives the advocates of war the opportunity to assert that the difference between them and us is only one of temporary expediency or personal appraisal, and our disagreement is then reduced to the fact that we consider war to be useless, while they consider it still useful. They readily concede that it may become unnecessary and even harmful – but only tomorrow and not today. Today they consider it necessary to perform on people these terrible blood-lettings which are called wars, and which are made only to satisfy the personal ambitions of a very small minority – to ensure power, honors, and riches to a small number of men to the detriment of the masses, whose natural credulity and superstitions these men exploit, together with the prejudices created and upheld by them.

Capitaine Gaston Mock.

Men of our Christian world in our time are like a man who has missed the right turning and becomes more and more convinced, the farther he goes, that he is going the wrong way. Yet the greater his doubts the quicker and more desperately does he hurry on, consoling himself with the thought that he must arrive somewhere. But the time comes when it is quite clear that the way along which he is going leads only to a precipice, which he begins to discern before him.

That is where Christian humanity stands in our time. We are presently guided in our private lives and in the lives of our separate states solely by desire for personal welfare for ourselves or our states, and we think to ensure this welfare by violence. It is quite evident that if we continue to live as we are doing, then the means for violence of man against man and state against state will inevitably increase. We shall first ruin ourselves more and more by expending a major portion of our productivity on armaments, and then we shall become more and more degenerate and depraved by killing the physically best men in wars.

If we do not change our way of life, this is as certain as it is mathematically certain that two non-parallel straight lines must meet. And not only is it certain theoretically, but in our time our feeling as well as our intelligence becomes convinced of it. The precipice we are approaching is already visible, and even the most simple, naive, and uneducated people cannot fail to see that, by arming our-selves increasingly against one another and slaughtering one another in war, we must inevitably come to mutual destruction, like spiders in ajar.

A sincere, serious, and rational man can now no longer console himself with the thought that matters can be mended, as was formerly supposed, by a univer-sal empire such as that of Rome, Charlemagne, or Napoleon; or by the medieval, spiritual power of the Pope; or by alliances; or by the political balance of a Euro-pean treaty and peaceful international tribunals; or, as some have thought, by an increase of military forces and the invention of new and more powerful weapons of destruction.

The organization of a universal empire or republic of European states is im-possible, for the different peoples will never wish to unite into one state. Shall we then organize international tribunals for the solution of international disputes? But who would impose obedience to the tribunal's decision on a contending party that had an army of millions of men? Disarmament? No one desires to begin it, or is able to do so. Shall we perhaps invent even more dreadful means of destruc-tion – balloons with bombs filled with suffocating gases, which men will shower on each other from above? Whatever may be invented, every state would furnish itself with similar weapons of destruction. And as the human cannon-fodder faced the bullets that succeeded sword and spear, and the shells, bombs, long-range guns, shrapnel, and torpedoes that succeeded bullets, so it will submit to bombs charged with suffocating gases scattered down upon it from the air.

The speeches of M. Muravëv and Professor Martens as to the Japanese war not conflicting with the Hague Peace Conference show more obviously than any-thing else to what an extent speech – the organ for the transmission of thought – is distorted amongst men of our time, and show that the capacity for clear, rational thinking is completely lost. Thought and speech are used not to guide human activity but to justify any activity, however criminal it may be. The late Boer war and the present Japanese war (which may at any moment expand into univer-sal slaughter) have proved this beyond all doubt. All anti-war discussions are as useless as an attempt to stop a dog-fight by an eloquent and convincing speech pointing out to the dogs that it would be better to share the piece of meat they are struggling over, rather than to bite one another and lose the piece of meat which is bound to be carried off by some passing non-combatant dog.

We are rushing on towards the precipice and cannot stop, but are tumbling over it. No rational man who reflects on the present position of humanity, and on what its future must inevitably be, can help seeing that there is no practical way out; that it is impossible to devise any alliance or organization that can save us from the destruction into which we are uncontrollably rushing.

Quite apart from the economic problems that become more and more com-plex, the mutual relations of states arming against one another and the wars that are ready at any moment to break out clearly indicate the unavoidable destruction awaiting so-called civilized humanity.

Then what is to be done?

CHAPTER VI

Jesus proclaimed a new society towards the close of his mission. Before his time, nations belonged to one or several masters and were their property like so many herds. Princes and grandees crushed the world with all the weight of their pride and their rapacity. Then Jesus came to put an end to this extreme disorder. He came to lift the bowed heads and to emancipate the slaves. He taught them that they are equal before God and are therefore free in regard to each other, that no one has any intrinsic power over his brothers, that the divine laws of equality and liberty are inviolable, and that power, rather than being a right, is a social duty, a service, a kind of bondage freely accepted for the welfare of all. Such is the society that Jesus established.

Is that what we now see in the world? Is that the doctrine that reigns on earth? Has it conquered the Gentiles? Are the rulers of nations the servants, or the masters, of their people? For eighteen centuries, generation after generation passes on the teaching of Christ and says that it believes in it. But what change is there in the world? The nations – crushed and suffering – are still awaiting the promised liberation, not because Christ's words were untrue or unreal, but because the people either did not understand that the fruits of the teaching must be secured by an effort of their own will, or because, numbed by their humiliations, they did not do the one thing that brings victory: they were not ready to die for the truth. But they will awaken; something is already stirring within them; they have heard a voice that cries: "Salvation draws nigh."

Lamennais.

To the glory of humanity, t must be said that the nineteenth century tends to approach a new path. Humanity has learned that laws and tribunals should exist for nations and that, because they are accomplished on a larger scale, crimes committed by nations against nations are not less hateful than crimes committed amongst individuals.

Quetelet.

All men are one in origin, one in the law that governs them, and one in the goal they are destined to attain. Your faith must be one, your actions one, and one the banner under which you contend. Acts, tears, and martyrdoms, form a language common to all men and which all men understand.

J. Mazzini.

No, I appeal to the revolt of the conscience of every man who has seen, or made, the blood of his fellow citizens flow. It is not enough that one single head should carry a burden as heavy as that of so many murders; as many heads as there are combatants would not be too many. In order to be responsible for the law of blood that they execute, it would be just that they should at least have understood it. But the best organizations that I advocate would in themselves be only temporary; for I repeat once more, that armies and war will only last a while. Notwithstanding the words of a sophist, which I have elsewhere controverted, it is not true that war, even against the foreigner, is *divine*. It is not true that *the earth is thirsting for blood*. War is accursed of God, and even those men who make it have a secret horror of it. The earth cries to heaven praying for fresh water in its rivers, and for the pure dew of its clouds.

Alfred de Vigny.

Men are easily coerced and made to obey, and mutually deprave one another by those two habits. Here stultification, there insolence, nowhere true human dignity.

V. P. Considerant.

If my soldiers were to begin to think, not one of them would remain in the army.

Frederick the Great.

Two thousand years ago John the Baptist, and after him Jesus, said to the people, "The time is fulfilled, and the Kingdom of God is at hand. Bethink yourselves (μετανοεῖτε) and believe in the Gospel." (Mark 1:15) "And if you do not bethink yourselves, you will all perish." (Luke 13:5)

But men did not listen, and the destruction foretold is already near at hand, as men of our time cannot but see. We are already perishing, and therefore we cannot close our ears to that means of salvation given of old, but new to us. We cannot but see that besides all the other calamities that flow from our evil and irrational life, military preparations alone and the wars resulting from them must inevitably destroy us. We cannot but see that all the practical means devised for escape from these evils are and must be ineffectual, and that the disastrous plight of nations arming themselves one against another must continually become worse. Therefore, the words of Jesus apply to us and to our time more than to anyone else or to any other time.

He said, "Bethink yourselves!" – that is, let every man interrupt his work and ask himself: "Who am I? From where have I come? And what is my vocation?" Having answered these questions, let him decide, according to the answer, whether what he does is in accord with his vocation. It is only necessary for each man of our world and time (each man acquainted with the essence of the Christian teaching) to interrupt his activity for a minute, to forget what people consider him to be – emperor, soldier, minister, or journalist – and to seriously ask himself who he is and what is his vocation, and he will at once doubt the utility, rightfulness, and reasonableness of his activity. "Before I am emperor, soldier, minister, or journalist," every man of our Christian world should say to himself, "before all else I am a man. I am an organic being sent by a higher will into a universe endless in time and space, where, after staying in it for an instant, I shall die and disappear from it. Therefore, all those personal, social, or even universal human aims, which I set before myself and which are set before me by men, are insignificant because of the brevity of my life as well as the illimitability of the life of the universe, and should be subordinated to that higher aim for the attainment of which I am sent into the world. That ultimate aim, owing to my limitations, is not understood by me but exists (as there must be a purpose in everything that exists), and my business is to be its tool. My vocation therefore is to be God's workman, fulfilling His work." And having understood his vocation in this way, every man of our world and time, from emperor to soldier, cannot help seeing with different eyes the duties that he has taken upon himself or that others have laid upon him.

"Before I was crowned and recognized as Emperor," the Emperor should say to himself, "before I undertook to fulfill the duties of head of the state, I promised by the very fact that I am alive to fulfill what is demanded of me by that higher will which sent me into life. I not only know those demands but I feel them in my heart. They consist, as is said in the Christian law, which I profess, in submitting to the will of God, and in fulfilling what it requires of me, namely, that I should love my neighbor, serve him, and do to him as I would wish him to do to me. Am I doing this by ruling men and ordering violence, executions, and most dreadful of all – wars?

"Men tell me that I ought to do this. But God says that I ought to do something quite different. And therefore, however much I may be told that as head of the state I must order deeds of violence, the levying of taxes, executions, and above all war – the killing of my fellow men – I do not wish to, and cannot, do these things."

And the soldier who is commanded to kill men should say the same thing to himself, and so should the politician who deems it his duty to prepare for war, and the journalist who incites men to war, and every man who has put to himself the questions of who he is and what is his vocation in life. And as soon as the head of the state ceases to direct war, the soldier to fight, the politician to prepare means for war, and the journalist to incite men thereto – then, without any new institutions, devices, balance of power, or tribunals, that hopeless position in which people have placed themselves not only as regards war but as regards all their other self-inflicted calamities will cease to exist.

Strange as this may seem, the surest and most certain deliverance for men from all their self-inflicted calamities, even the most dreadful of them – war – is attainable not by any external general measures but by that simple appeal to the consciousness of each individual man which was presented by Jesus nineteen hundred years ago: that every man should bethink himself and ask himself who he is, why he lives, and what he should and should not do.

CHAPTER VII

There is a widespread impression abroad that religion may not be a permanent element in human nature. Many are telling us that it is a phase of thought, of feeling, of life, peculiar to the early and comparatively uncultivated stages of man's career, and that it is something which civilized man will progressively outgrow and at last leave behind... I do not think we need be especially troubled over this problem. We ought to be able to look at it dispassionately, because if religion is only superstition, why then of course it ought to be outgrown... If on the other hand religion is divine, if it is essential to the highest and noblest human life, then criticism and question will only verify this fact... If you find some mark on a coin, if you find it on every one of the coins, you feel perfectly certain that there is some reality in the coin-stamping die that accounts for such a mark. It was not there for nothing; it did not simply happen.

So wherever you find any universal or permanently characteristic quality in human nature, or any other nature for that matter, you may feel perfectly certain that there is something real in the universe that corresponds to it and called it out.

You find man, then, universally a religious being. You find him everywhere believing that he is confronted with an invisible universe. On any theory you choose to hold about this universe, it has made us what we are. There must be – unless the universe is a lie – a reality corresponding to that which is universal and permanent and real in ourselves, because this universe has called these things into being and has made them what they are.

Minot J. Savage, The Passing and the Permanent in Religion.

The religious element, contemplated from that elevated standpoint, becomes thus the highest and noblest factor in man's education, the greatest potency in his civilization, while effete creeds and political selfishness are the greatest obstacles to human advance. Statecraft and priestcraft are the very opposite of religion... Our study here has shown the religious substance everywhere to be identical, eternal, and divine, permeating the human heart wherever it throbs, feels, and meditates... The logical results of our researches all point to the identical basis of the great religions, to the one doctrine unfolding since the dawn of humanity to this day... Deep at the bottom of all the creeds flows the stream of the one eternal revelation, *the one religion*, the "word of God to the mind of man."

Let the Parsee wear his taavids, the Jew his phylacteries, the Christian his cross, and the Muslim his crescent; but let them all remember that these are forms and emblems, while the practical essence is: "You shall love your neighbor as yourself." This is equally emphasized and accentuated by Manu, Zoroaster, Buddha, Abraham, Moses, Socrates, Hillel, Jesus, Paul, and Mohammed.

Maurice Fleugel.

No true society can exist without a common faith and common purpose. Political activity is their application, and religion supplies their principle. The will of the majority rules where this common faith is lacking, showing itself in constant instability and the oppression of others. It is possible to coerce without God, but not to persuade. Without God, the majority will be a tyrant, but not an educator of the people.

What we need, what the people need, and what the age is crying for that it may find an issue from the slough of selfishness, doubt, and negation in which it is submerged – is faith, in which our souls, ceasing to wander in search of individual ends, can march together in consciousness of one origin, one law, and one goal. Every strong faith that arises on the ruins of old and outlived beliefs changes the existing social order, for every strong faith inevitably influences all departments of human activity.

In different forms and different degrees, humanity repeats the words of the Lord's Prayer: "Thy kingdom come on earth as in heaven."

Mazzini.

A man may regard himself as an animal among animals, living for the passing day; or he may consider himself as a member of a family, a society, or a nation, living for centuries; or he may and even must (for reason irresistibly prompts him to this) consider himself as part of the whole infinite universe existing eternally. And therefore a reasonable man, besides his relation to the immediate facts of life, must always set up his relation to the whole immense Infinite in time and space, conceived as one whole. And such establishment of man's relation to that whole of which he feels himself to be a part, and from which he draws guidance for his actions, is what has been called and is called religion. And therefore religion always has been, and cannot cease to be, a necessary and indispensable condition of the life of a reasonable man and of all reasonable humanity.

Leo Tolstoy, What is Religion?

Religion (regarded objectively) is the recognition of all our duties as the commands of God... There is only one true religion, though there may be various faiths.

Kant.

The evil from which men of our time are suffering comes from the fact that the majority of them live without what alone affords a rational guidance for human activity, namely religion. This is not a religion that consists in a belief in dogmas or the fulfillment of rites affording a pleasant diversion, consolation, or stimulation, but a religion that establishes the relation of man to the All, to God. Such a religion therefore gives a general higher direction to all human activity, and without it people stand on the plane of animals, or even lower than animals. This evil, leading men to inevitable destruction, has shown itself with particular strength in our time. Men, having lost a rational guidance in life and having directed all their efforts to discoveries and improvements chiefly in the sphere of technical knowledge, have developed enormous power over the forces of nature, but lacking guidance for its rational application have naturally used it for the satisfaction of their lower animal impulses.

Bereft of religion, men possessing enormous power over the forces of nature are like children to whom gunpowder or explosive gas has been given as a plaything. Considering this power that men of our time possess, and the way they use it, one feels that their degree of moral development does not really qualify them to use railways, steam-power, electricity, telephones, photography, wireless telegraphy, or even to manufacture iron and steel, for they use all these things merely to satisfy their desires, amuse themselves, become dissipated, and destroy one another.

Then what is to be done? Discard all these improvements, all this power mankind has acquired? Forget what it has learned? That is impossible! However harmfully these mental acquisitions are used, they are still acquisitions and men cannot forget them. Alter those combinations of nations which have been formed during centuries and establish new ones? Invent new institutions that would prevent the minority from deceiving and exploiting the majority? Diffuse knowledge? All this has been tried and is being tried with great fervor. All these supposed improvements supply a chief means to distract and divert men's attention from the consciousness of inevitable destruction. The boundaries of states are altered, institutions are changed, and knowledge is disseminated, but with these other boundaries, other organizations, and increased knowledge men remain the same beasts ready at any moment to tear each other to pieces. Or, they remain the same slaves they always have been and always will be, as long as they continue to be guided, not by religious consciousness, but by passions, theories, and external suggestions.

Man has no choice. He must be the slave of the most unscrupulous and insolent among slaves, or else a servant of God, because there is but one way for man to be free: by uniting his will with the will of God. Some people bereft of religion repudiate religion itself. Others regard as religion those external perverted forms that have superseded it, and guided only by their personal desires – by fear, human laws, or chiefly by mutual hypnotism – they cannot cease to be animals or slaves. No external efforts can release them from this state, for religion alone makes man free.

And most men of our time lack it.

CHAPTER VIII

Do not that which your conscience condemns, and say not that which does not agree with truth. Fulfill this, the most important duty, and you will have fulfilled all the object of your life.

No one can coerce your will; it is accessible neither to thief nor robber. Desire not that which is unreasonable; desire general welfare, and not personal as do the majority of men. The object of life is not to be on the side of the majority, but to escape finding oneself in the ranks of the insane…

Remember that there is a God who desires neither praise nor glory from men created in his image, but rather that they, guided by the understanding given them, should in their actions become like unto him. A fig tree is true to its purpose; so is the dog, and so also are bees. Then is it possible that man shall not fulfill his vocation? But, alas, these great and sacred truths vanish from your memory. The bustle of daily life, war, unreasonable fear, spiritual debility, and the habit of being a slave stifle them…

A small branch cut from the main branch has become thereby separated from the whole tree. A man in enmity with another man is severed from the whole of mankind. But a branch is cut off by another's hand, whereas man estranges himself from his neighbor by hatred and spite, without knowing that thereby he tears himself away from the whole of mankind. But the Divinity, having called men into common life as brothers, has endowed them with freedom to become reconciled to each other after dissension.

Marcus Aurelius.

Enlightenment is the escape of man from his own childishness, which he himself maintains. The childishness consists in his incapacity to use his reason without another's guidance. He himself maintains this childishness when it is the result of an insufficiency, not of reason, but of the decision and manliness to use it without another's guidance. *"Sapere aude!"*

Have the manliness to use your own reason. This is the motto of enlightenment.

Kant.

One must extricate the religion Jesus professed from the religion of which Jesus is the object. And when we have laid our finger upon the state of conscience that is the original cell, the basis of the eternal Gospel, we must hold onto it.

As the faint illuminations of a village festival or the miserable candles of a procession disappear before the great marvel of the sun's light, so also small local miracles, accidental and doubtful, will flicker out before the law of the world of the Spirit, before the incomparable spectacle of human history guided by God.

Amiel, Fragments d'un journal intimé.

I recognize the following proposition as needing no proof: all by which man thinks he can please God, save a good life, is merely religious error and superstition.

Kant.

In reality there is only one means of worshipping God: it is by the fulfillment of one's duties, and by acting in accord with the laws of reason.

G. C. Lichtenberg.

"But in order to abolish the evil from which we are suffering," those who are preoccupied by various practical activities will say, "it would be necessary not for a few men only, but for all men to bethink themselves, and having done so to understand the vocation of their lives to lie in the fulfillment of the will of God and the service of their neighbor. Is that possible?'

Not only is it possible, I reply, but it is impossible that it should not be so.

It is impossible for men not to bethink themselves – impossible, that is, for each man not to put to himself the questions of who he is and why he lives. Man, as a rational being, cannot live without a knowledge of why he lives, and has always put that question to himself. And according to the degree of his development, he has always answered it in his religious teaching. In our time, the inner contradiction in which men feel themselves to be presents this question with particular insistence and demands an answer. It is impossible for men of our time to answer this question otherwise than by recognizing the law of life to lie in loving others and being in their service. This is the only rational answer as to the meaning of human life, this answer was expressed nineteen hundred years ago in the Christian religion, and it is known in the same way to the great majority of all mankind.

This answer lives in a latent state in the consciousness of all people of the Christian world of our time. There are only two reasons why it does not openly express itself and serve as guidance for our lives. On the one hand, those who enjoy the greatest authority – the so-called scientists – being under the coarse delusion that religion is a temporary stage in the development of mankind, which they have outgrown, and under the delusion that men can live without religion, impress this error on those of the masses who are beginning to be educated. On the other hand, those in power consciously or unconsciously (being themselves under the delusion that the Church faith is the Christian religion) try to support and promote in people the crude superstitions that are given out as the Christian religion.

If only these two deceptions were destroyed, true religion, which is already latent in people of our time, would become evident and obligatory.

To bring this about it is necessary that, on the one hand, men of science should understand that the principle of the brotherhood of all men, and the rule of not doing to others what one does not wish for oneself, is not a casual conception. It is not one of a multitude of human theories that can be subordinated to other considerations. Instead, it is an indubitable principle standing higher than other perceptions and flowing from the unalterable relations of man to the eternal – to God. It is religion, all religion, and therefore always obligatory.

On the other hand, it is necessary that those who consciously or unconsciously preach crude superstitions under the guise of Christianity should understand that all these dogmas, sacraments, and rites, which they support and preach, are not harmless as they suppose. They are in the highest degree harmful, concealing from men that one religious truth which is expressed in the fulfillment of God's will: the brotherhood of man and service of man. The rule of doing to others as you wish others to do to you is not *one* of the prescriptions of the Christian religion but is the *whole* of practical religion, as is said in the Gospels.

That men of our time should uniformly place before themselves the question of the meaning of life, and uniformly answer it, it is only necessary for those who regard themselves as enlightened to cease to think and impress on others (a) that religion is atavistic – the survival of a savage past – and (b) that for the good life of men a spreading of education is sufficient, that is, the spread of very miscellaneous knowledge which is somehow to bring men to justice and a moral life.[4] These men should understand instead that religion is vital for the good life of humanity, and that this religion already exists and lives in the consciousness of the men of our time. Authorities who are intentionally and unintentionally stupefying the people by Church superstitions should cease to do so, and should recognize that what is important and obligatory in Christianity is not baptism, or the sacraments, or the profession of dogmas, and so forth, but only love of God and one's neighbor, and the fulfillment of the command to act towards others as you wish others to act towards you. In this is all the law and the prophets.

If only this were understood both by pseudo-Christians and by men of science, and these simple, clear, and necessary truths were preached to children and to the uneducated, as they now preach their complicated, confused, and unnecessary theories, all men would uniformly understand the meaning of their lives and recognize the same duties as flowing from that meaning therefrom.

---

[4] See in the essay *Religion and Morality* (vol. xii of the Centenary Edition, p. 192 contains Tolstoy's reply to Thomas Huxley's Romanes Lecture in 1894.–A.M.

CHAPTER IX

(A letter from a Russian peasant who refused military service)

On October 15th, 1895, I was called up for conscription. When my turn came to draw the lot I said I would not do so. The officials looked at me, consulted together, and asked me why I refused.

I answered that it was because I was not going either to take the oath or to carry a gun.

They said that that would be seen to later, but now I must draw the lot.

I refused once more. Then they told the village Elder to draw the lot. He did so and number 674 came out. It was written down.

The military commander entered, called me into his office, and asked, "Who taught you all this – that you don't want to take the oath?"

"I learned it myself by reading the Gospel," I answered.

"I don't think you are able to understand the Gospel," he replied. "Everything there is incomprehensible. To understand it one has to learn a great deal."

To this I said that Jesus did not teach anything incomprehensible, for even the simplest uneducated people understood his teaching.

Then he told a soldier to take me to the barracks. I went to the kitchen with him and we had dinner there.

After dinner they asked me why I had not taken the oath.

"Because it is said in the Gospel, 'Swear not at all,'" I replied.

They were astonished. Then they asked me, "Is that really in the Gospel? Find it for us."

I found the passage, read it out, and they listened.

"But even if it is there," they said, "you can't refuse to take the oath or you'll be tortured."

"He who loses his earthly life will inherit eternal life," I replied…

On the 20th I was placed in a row with other young soldiers, and the military rules were explained to us. I told them that I would fulfill nothing of this. They asked why.

I said, "Because as a Christian I will not bear arms or defend myself from enemies, for Christ commanded us to love even our enemies."

"But are you the only Christian?" they asked. "Why, we are all Christians!"

"I know nothing about others," I replied. "I only know for myself that Jesus told us to do what I am now doing."

The commander said, "If you won't drill, I'll let you rot in prison."

To this I replied, "Do what you like with me, but I won't serve."

Today a commission examined me. The general said to the officers, "What opinions has this suckling got hold of that he refuses service? Millions serve, and he alone refuses. Have him well flogged; then he will change his views..."

Olkhovík was transported to the Amur. On the steamer everybody fasted during Lent, but he refused. The soldiers asked him why. He explained. Another soldier (Seredá) joined in the conversation. Olkhovík opened the Gospel and began to read the fifth chapter of Matthew. Having read it, he said, "Jesus forbids the oath, courts of justice, and war, but all this is done among us and is considered legitimate." A crowd of soldiers had collected around, and remarked that Seredá was not wearing a cross on his neck. "Where is your cross?" they asked.

"In my box," he answered.

They asked again, "Why don't you wear it?"

"Because I love Jesus," he replied, "and so I can't wear the thing on which he was crucified."

Then two non-commissioned officers came up and began talking to Seredá. They asked, "How is it that not long ago you used to fast, but now you have taken off your cross?"

He replied, "Because I was then in the dark and did not see the light, but now I have begun to read the Gospel and have learned that a Christian need not do all that."

Then they asked, "Does this mean that, like Olkhovík, you won't serve?"

"Yes," he replied.

They asked why, and he answered, "Because I am a Christian,

and Christians must not take arms against men."

Seredá was arrested and, together with Olkhovík, was exiled to the province of Yakútsk, where they now are.

From The Letters of P. V. Olkhovík.

On January 27th, 1894, in the Vorónezh prison hospital, a man named Drozhín, formerly a village teacher in Kursk province, died of pneumonia. His body was thrown into a grave in the prison cemetery like the bodies of all the criminals who die in the prison. Yet he was one of the saintliest, purest, and most truthful men that ever lived.

In August 1891 he was called up for conscription, but, considering all men to be his brothers and regarding murder and violence as the greatest sins against conscience and the will of God, he refused to be a soldier or to bear arms. Also, considering it a sin to surrender his will into the power of others who might demand evil actions of him, he refused to take the oath. Men whose lives are founded on violence and murder condemned him first to one year's solitary confinement in Khárkov, but later he was transferred to the Vorónezh penal battalion where for fifteen months he was tortured by cold, hunger, and solitary confinement. Finally, when consumption developed from his incessant sufferings and privations and he was recognized as unfit for military service, he was transferred to the civil prison where he was to remain confined for another nine years. But while being transferred from the penal battalion to the prison on an extremely frosty day, the police officials neglected to furnish him with a warm coat. The party remained for a long time in the street in front of the police station, and this caused him to catch such a cold that pneumonia set in, from which he died twenty-two days later.

The day before his death, Drozhín said to the doctor, "Though I have not lived long, I die with a consciousness of having acted in accord with my convictions and my conscience. Others of course may judge about this better than I can. Perhaps… No, I think that I am right," he concluded.

From The Life and Death of Drozhín.

Put on the full armor of God so that you can take your stand against the devil's schemes. For our struggle is not against flesh and blood, but against the rulers, against the authorities, against the powers of this dark world and against the spiritual forces of evil in the heavenly realms. Therefore put on the full armor of God, so that when the day of evil comes, you may be able to stand your ground, and after you have done everything, to stand. Stand firm then, with the belt of truth buckled around your waist, with the breastplate of righteousness in place.

Ephesians vi. 11-14.

But I shall be asked, "How are we to act now – immediately – among ourselves in Russia at this moment, when our foes are already attacking us, killing our people, and threatening us? How is a Russian soldier, officer, general, Tsar, or private individual, to act? Are we really to let our enemies ruin our dominions, seize the products of our labor, carry off prisoners, and kill our men? What are we to do now that this thing has begun?"

"But before the work of war began," every man who has reflected should reply, "before all else, the work of my life had begun." The work of my life has nothing to do with recognition of the rights of the Chinese, Japanese, or Russians to Port Arthur. The work of my life consists in fulfilling the will of Him who sent me into this life. And that will is known to me. That will is that I should love my neighbor and serve him. Then why should I – following temporary, casual demands that are cruel and irrational – deviate from the eternal and changeless law of my whole life? If there is a God, He will not ask me when I die (which may happen at any moment) whether I retained Chinnampo with its timber stores, or Port Arthur, or even that conglomeration which is called the Russian Empire, which He did not entrust to my care. He will ask me what I have done with that life which He has put at my disposal. Did I use it for the purpose for which it was intended and under whose conditions it was entrusted to me? Have I fulfilled His law?

To this question as to what is to be done now that war has begun, for me, a man who understands his vocation, whatever position I may occupy, there can be no other answer than this: that whatever the circumstances may be, whether the war has begun or not, whether thousands of Russians or Japanese have been killed, whether not only Port Arthur but St. Petersburg and Moscow have been captured – I cannot act otherwise than as God demands of me, and that therefore I as a man cannot either directly or indirectly, whether by organizing, helping, or inciting to it, take part in war. *I cannot, I do not wish to, and I will not.* I do not and cannot know what will happen immediately or later from my ceasing to do what is contrary to the will of God, but I believe that nothing can follow from fulfilling the will of God but what is good for me and for all men.

You speak with horror of what would happen if we Russians at once ceased to fight and yielded to the Japanese all that they wish of us. But if it is true that the salvation of mankind from brutalization and self-destruction lies solely in the establishment among men of true religion, demanding that we should love our neighbor and serve him (with which it is impossible to disagree), then every war, every hour of war, and my participation in it only renders the realization of this only possible means of salvation more difficult and remote. Even looking at it from your precarious point of view – appraising actions by their presumed consequences – even so, a yielding by the Russians to the Japanese of all that they desire of us, apart from the unquestionable advantage of ending the ruin and slaughter, would be an advance toward the only means of saving mankind from destruction, whereas the continuance of the war, however it may end, would hinder that only means of salvation.

"But even if this were so," people reply, "wars can cease only when all men, or the majority of them, refuse to participate in them. The refusal of one man, whether he is Tsar or soldier, would only unnecessarily ruin his life, without the least advantage to anyone. If the Russian Tsar were now to renounce the war, he would be dethroned or perhaps killed to get rid of him. If an ordinary man were to refuse military service, he would be sent to a penal battalion or perhaps shot. Why then uselessly throw away one's life, which might be of use to society?" This is usually said by those who do not think of the vocation of their whole life, and therefore do not understand it.

But this is not what is said and felt by a man who understands the purpose of his life, that is, by a religious man. Such a one is guided in his activity, not by the conjectural consequences of his actions, but by the consciousness of the purpose of his life. A factory workman goes to the factory and in it does the work allotted to him without considering what will be the consequence of his work. In the same way a soldier acts, carrying out the will of his commanders. So acts a religious man, doing the work prescribed to him by God without arguing as to just what will come of his work. And so for a religious man there is no question as to whether many or few men act as he does, or of what may happen to him if he does what he should do. He knows that nothing can happen besides life and death, and that life and death are in the hands of God, whom he obeys.

A religious man acts so and not otherwise, not because he wishes to act thus or because it is advantageous to him or to others, but because, believing that his life is in the hands of God, he cannot do otherwise. In this lies the speciality of the activity of religious men. And so the salvation of men from the ills they inflict upon themselves will be accomplished only to the extent to which they are guided in their lives, not by advantages or arguments, but by religious consciousness.

CHAPTER X

Men of God are that hidden salt which conserves the world, for the things of the world are conserved only in so far as the Divine salt does not lose its power. "But if the salt has lost its savor, with what can it be salted? It is thenceforth good for nothing but to be cast out and trodden underfoot by men… He who has ears to hear, let him hear." As for us, we are persecuted when God gives the tempter the power to persecute, but when He does not wish to subject us to sufferings, we enjoy wonderful peace even in this world which hates us, and we rely on the protection of Him who said, "Be of good cheer, for I have overcome the world."

Celsus also says, "It is impossible that all the inhabitants of Asia, Europe, and Libya, Greeks as well as barbarians, should follow one and the same law. To think so," he says, "means to understand nothing." But we say that not only is it possible, but that the day will come when all reasonable beings will unite under one law. For the Word or Reason will subdue all reasonable beings and transform them into its own perfection.

There are bodily diseases and wounds that no doctoring can cure, but it is not so with the ailments of the soul. There is no evil the cure of which is impossible for supreme Reason, which is God.

Origen, *Origen, Against Celsus.*

I feel the force stirring within me, which in time will reform the world. It does not push or obtrude, but I am conscious of it drawing gently and irresistibly at my vitals. And I see that as I am attracted, so I begin unaccountably to attract others.

I draw them and they in turn draw me, and we recognize a tendency to group ourselves anew. Get in touch with the great central magnet, and you will yourself become a magnet. And as more and more of us find our bearings and exert our powers, gradually the new world will take shape. We become indeed legislators of the divine law, receiving it from God Himself, and human laws shrink and dry up before us.

I asked the force within my soul, "Who are you?" And it answered and said, "I am Love, the Lord of Heaven, and I would be called Love, the Lord of Earth. I am the mightiest of all the heavenly hosts, and I have come to create the state that is to be."

Ernest Crosby, Plain Talk in Psalm and Parable.

One can say with certainty that the kingdom of God has come to us when the principle of the gradual transformation of the church faith into a universal rational religion is found openly established anywhere, though the complete realization of that kingdom may still be infinitely far from us – for this principle, like a developing and then multiplying germ, already contains all which must enlighten and take possession of the world.

In the life of the universe a thousand years are as one day. We must labor patiently for this realization, and wait for it.

Kant.

When I speak to you about God, do not think that I am speaking to you about some object made of gold or silver. The God of whom I speak, you feel in your soul. You bear Him in yourself, and by your impure thoughts and loathsome acts you defile His image in your soul. You refrain from doing anything that is unseemly in the presence of a golden idol, which you regard as God, but in the presence of that God who sees and hears all that is within you, you do not even blush when you yield yourself to your disgusting thoughts and actions.

If only we remembered that God in us is the witness of all that we do and think, we should cease to sin, and God would constantly abide in us. Let us then remember God, and think and talk of Him as often as possible.

Epictetus.

"But how about the enemies who are attacking us?"

"Love your enemies and you will have none," is said in the *Teaching of the Twelve Apostles.* And this answer is not mere words, as those may imagine who are accustomed to think that the injunction to love one's enemies is something rhetorical and signifies not what it says but something else. It is the indication of a very clear and definite activity and of its consequences.

To love one's enemies – the Japanese, the Chinese, "those yellow people" towards whom erring men are now trying to excite our hatred – to love them does not mean to kill them in order to have a right to poison them with opium, as was done by the English[5]; or to kill them in order to seize their land, as was done by the French, the Russians, and the Germans; or to bury them alive as punishment

---

[5] "The public conscience was wounded by a war with China in 1839 on its refusal to allow the smuggling of opium into its dominions." J. R. Green, (*A Short History of the English People*).–A.M.

for injuring roads, or to tie them together by their hair and drown them in the Amur, as the Russians did.

"A disciple is not above his master... It is enough for a disciple that he is as his master."

To love the "yellow people," whom we call our foes, does not mean teaching them, under the name of Christianity, absurd superstitions about the fall of man, redemption, resurrection, and so on. It does not mean teaching them the art of deceiving and killing people, but teaching them justice, unselfishness, compassion, and love, and that not in words but by the example of our own good lives.

But what have we done, and are we doing to them?

If we did indeed love our enemies, if even now we began to love our enemies the Japanese, we should have no enemy,

So, strange as it may appear to people occupied with military plans and preparations, diplomatic considerations, administrative, financial, and economic measures, revolutionary and socialistic sermons, and various unnecessary sciences, by which they think to free mankind from its calamities. The delivery of man, not only from the calamities of war, but from all his self-inflicted ills, will be effected, not through emperors or kings instituting peace unions, not by those who would dethrone kings or limit them by constitutions, not by replacing monarchies with republics, not by peace conferences, not by the accomplishment of socialistic programs, not by victories or defeats on land or sea, not by libraries or universities, and not by those futile mental exercises which are now called science, but only by there being more and more of those simple men like the Doukhobors, Drozhín, and Olkhovík in Russia, the Nazarenes in Austria, Condatier in France, Tervey in Holland, and others who set themselves the aim, not of external alterations of life, but of their own most faithful fulfillment of the will of Him who sent them into life, and direct all their powers to that fulfillment. Only such people, realizing the Kingdom of God in themselves, in their souls, will without aiming directly at that purpose, establish that external Kingdom of God which every human soul desires.

Salvation will come about only in this one way and not by any other. And what is now being done by those who, ruling others, instill into them religious and patriotic superstitions, exciting them to exclusiveness, hatred, and murder – as well as by those who provoke men to violent external revolution to free them from enslavement and oppression, or think that the acquisition of very much incidental, and for the most part unnecessary, knowledge will of itself bring men to a good life – all this, distracting men from what alone they need, merely removes them farther from the possibility of salvation.

The evil from which people of the Christian world suffer is that they are deprived of true religion.

Some people, convinced of the discord between existing religion and the state of mental, scientific development attained by humanity in our time, have decided in general that no religion whatever is necessary. They live without religion and preach the uselessness of any religion whatever. Others, holding to the distorted form of the Christian religion that is now preached, also live without religion, professing empty external forms that cannot serve as guidance for men's lives.

Yet a religion which answers to the demands of our time exists, is known to all men, and lives in a latent state in the hearts of men of the Christian world. For this religion to become evident to and binding upon all men, it is only necessary that educated men – the leaders of the masses – should understand that religion is necessary to man, that men cannot live good lives without religion, and that what they call science cannot replace religion. And men in power who support the old empty forms of religion should understand that what they support and preach as religion is not only not religion, but is the chief obstacle to people's assimilating the true religion, which they already know and which alone can save them from their miseries.

The only true means of man's salvation consists in merely ceasing to do what hinders men from making the true religion, which lives in their consciousness, their own.

CHAPTER XI

A horrible and shocking thing has happened in the land: the prophets prophecy lies, the priests rule by their own authority, and my people love it this way. But what will you do in the end?

Jeremiah v:30-31.

He has blinded their eyes and deadened their hearts, so they can neither see with their eyes, nor understand with their hearts, nor turn – and I would heal them.

John xii:40.

If a traveler were to see a people on some far-off island whose houses were protected by loaded cannon and around those houses sentinels patrolled night and day, he could not help thinking that the island was inhabited by brigands. Is it not thus with the European states? How little influence has religion on people, and how far we still are from true religion.

Lichtenberg.

I was finishing this article when news came of the destruction of six hundred innocent lives near Port Arthur. It would seem that the useless suffering and death of these unfortunate, deluded men, who have uselessly suffered a dreadful death, ought to bring to their senses those who were the cause of this destruction. I am not alluding to Makárov and other officers. All those men knew what they were doing and why, and voluntarily, for personal advantage or for ambition, did what they did, screening themselves under the lie of patriotism, which is obvious but is not exposed merely because it is universal. I mention those unfortunate men drawn from all parts of Russia who, by the help of religious fraud and under fear of punishment, were torn from their honest, reasonable, useful, and laborious family life and driven to the other end of the earth, placed on a cruel and senseless slaughtering machine, and torn to bits or drowned in a distant sea together with that stupid machine, without any need or any possibility of receiving any advantage from all their privations, efforts, and sufferings, and the death that overtook them.

In 1830, during the Polish war, Adjutant Vilejinsky, sent to St. Petersburg by Klopitsky, in a conversation carried on in French with Dibitch, replied to the latter's demands that the Russian troops should enter Poland:

"Monsieur le Maréchal, I think that it is quite impossible for the Polish nation to accept the manifesto with such a condition."

"Believe me, the Emperor will make no concession."

"Then I foresee that unhappily there will be war, much blood will be shed, and there will be many unfortunate victims."

"Don't believe it! At most, ten thousand men will perish on the two sides. That is all,"[6] said Dibitch in his German accent, quite confident that he, together with another man as cruel and alien to Russian and Polish life as himself (Nicholas I) had a right to condemn or not to condemn to death ten or a hundred thousand Russians and Poles.

One hardly believes that this could have been, so senseless and dreadful is it, and yet it was. Sixty thousand supporters of families perished by the will of those men. And the same thing is taking place now.

To keep the Japanese out of Manchuria and to drive them out of Korea, not ten but fifty thousand and more will in all probability be required. I do not know whether Nicholas II and Kuropátkin say in so many words, as Dibitch did, that *not more than fifty thousand lives* will be needed for this on the Russian side alone, *and only* that. But they think it and cannot but think it, because what they are doing speaks for itself. Those unfortunate and deluded Russian peasants, now being transported by the thousand in an unceasing flow to the Far East, are those same *not more than fifty thousand* living Russians whom Nicholas Románov and Alexéy Kuropátkin have decided to sacrifice. They will be killed in support of those stupidities, robberies, and nastinesses of all kinds that were being committed in China and Korea by immoral, ambitious men, now quietly sitting in their palaces and awaiting fresh glory and fresh advantage and profit from the slaughter of those fifty thousand unfortunate defrauded Russian working men who are guilty of nothing and gain nothing by their sufferings and death. Enormous sums are spent to take other people's land, to which the Russians have no right, which has been stolen from its legitimate owners, and which in reality the Russians do not need – as well as for certain shady dealings undertaken by speculators who wished to profit from other people's forests in Korea. This spent money represents a great part of the labor of the whole Russian people, while future generations of that people are being bound by debts, its best workmen are being withdrawn from labor, and scores of thousands of its sons are being mercilessly doomed to death. And the destruction of these unfortunate men has already begun. More than this, those who have hatched the war manage it so badly and carelessly, and all is so unexpected and unprepared that, as one paper remarks, Russia's chief chance of success lies in the fact that it has inexhaustible human material. Those who send scores of thousands of Russian men to their deaths rely on this!

It is plainly said that the regrettable reverses of our fleet must be compensated

---

[6] Vilejinsky adds, "The Field Marshal did not then think that more than sixty thousand of the Russians alone would perish in that war, not so much from the enemy's fire as from disease, and that he himself would be among the number."

for on land. In plain language this means that, if the authorities have managed things badly on sea and by their carelessness have wasted not only the nation's riches but thousands of lives, we must make up for this by condemning to death several more scores of thousands on land!

Crawling locusts cross rivers in this way. The lower layers are drowned until the bodies of the drowned form a bridge over which those above can pass. This is how the Russian people are now disposed of. The first lower layer is already beginning to drown, showing the way for other thousands who will likewise perish.

And do the originators, the instigators and directors of this dreadful business, begin to understand their sin and their crime? Not in the least. They are fully persuaded that they have fulfilled and are fulfilling their duty, and they are proud of their activity. They talk of the loss of the brave Makárov, who as all agree was able to kill men very cleverly, and they deplore the loss of an excellent machine of slaughter that cost so many millions of rubles, which has now been sunk. They discuss how to find another murderer as capable as poor misguided Makárov, they invent new and even more efficacious tools of slaughter, and all the guilty people engaged in this dreadful work, from the Tsar to the humblest journalist, call with one voice for new insanities and cruelties, and for an intensification of brutality and hatred of one's fellow men.

"Makárov was not alone in Russia and every admiral placed in his position will follow in his steps and will continue the plan and the idea of him who has perished nobly in the strife," writes the *Novoe Vremya*.

"Let us earnestly pray to God for those who have laid down their lives for the sacred Fatherland, not doubting for one moment that the Fatherland will give us fresh sons equally valorous for the further struggle, and will find in them an inexhaustible supply of strength for a worthy completion of the work," writes the *Petersburg Vedomosti*.

"A virile nation will form no other conclusion from the defeat, however unprecedented, than that we must continue, develop, and conclude the strife. We shall find in ourselves fresh strength, and new heroes of the spirit will appear," writes the *Russ*. And so on.

And so, murder and every kind of crime continue with yet greater fury. People are enthusiastic about the martial spirit of the volunteers who, having unexpectedly come upon fifty of their fellow men, cut them all to pieces, or who occupied a village and massacred its whole population, or who hung or shot those accused of spying – that is, of doing the very thing which is regarded as indispensable and is constantly being done on our side. News of these crimes is reported in pompous telegrams to their chief director, the Tsar, who sends his valorous troops his blessing for the continuation of such deeds.

Is it not clear that if there is a salvation from this state of things, it is only one: that one which Jesus teaches? "Seek first the kingdom of God and his righteousness" (that which is within you), and all the rest – all the practical welfare for which man is striving – will be realized of itself.

Such is the law of life. Practical welfare is not attained when man strives for it. On the contrary, such striving for the most part removes man from the attainment of what he seeks. This practical welfare is only incidentally attained when, without thinking of it, men strive towards the most perfect fulfillment of that which they regard as right before God, the Source and Law of their lives.

There is only one true salvation for men: the fulfillment of the will of God by each individual within himself, in that portion of the universe which alone is subject to his power. In this is the chief and sole vocation of every individual, and at the same time the only means by which every individual can influence others. To this, and only to this, all the efforts of every man should be directed.

April 17th, o. s., 1904.

CHAPTER XII

I had only just sent off the last pages of this article on war, when the terrible news arrived of a fresh iniquity committed against the Russian people by those men who, crazed by power and lacking any sense of responsibility, have assumed the right to dispose of them. Again those coarse and servile slaves of slaves – the various generals – decked out in a variety of motley garments, have (either to distinguish themselves, or to spite one another, or to earn the right to add another little star, decoration, or ribbon, to their ridiculous and ostentatious dress, or from sheer stupidity and carelessness) destroyed thousands of those honorable, kindly, laborious working men who provide them with food, and destroyed them with terrible sufferings. Once again this iniquity not only fails to make its perpetrators reflect or repent, but they only tell us how still more men and still more families (both Russian and Japanese) may be killed, mutilated, or ruined with the greatest speed.

More than this, those guilty of these evil deeds, wishing to prepare people for still more of them, do not confess (what is evident to everybody) that, even from their patriotic military point of view, the Russians have suffered a shameful defeat. Instead, they even try to instill into frivolous minds a belief that those unfortunate Russian peasants have performed a heroic feat, since those who could not run away were killed and those who did run away remained alive. Those peasants were led into a trap like cattle into a slaughterhouse, and several thousand were killed and maimed simply because one general did not understand what another general had said.

The drowning of many peaceful Japanese by one of those terrible, immoral, cruel men, extolled as generals and admirals, is also described as a great and valorous achievement that must gladden the hearts of the Russian people. And in all the papers this horrible incitement to murder appears:

"Let the two thousand Russians killed on the Yalu, together with the maimed Retvizán, her sister ships, and our lost torpedo-boats, teach our cruisers what devastating destruction they must wreak upon the shores of base Japan. She has sent her soldiers to shed Russian blood and no mercy must be shown her. It is impossible to sentimentalize now; it would be sinful. We must fight! We must deal such heavy blows that their memory will freeze the treacherous hearts of the Japanese. Now is the time for our cruisers to put to sea and reduce their towns to ashes, and to rush like a terrible calamity along their beautiful shores."

"There has been enough of sentimentality!"

So the frightful work goes on: looting, violence, murder, hypocrisy, theft, and, above all, the most fearful deceit and the perversion of both the Christian and the Buddhist religions.

The Tsar, the man chiefly responsible, continues to hold reviews of his troops, thanks them, rewards and encourages them, and issues an edict calling up the reserves. Again and again his loyal subjects humbly lay their possessions and their lives at the feet of their adored monarch, but these are only words. In reality, desiring to distinguish themselves before each other in actual deeds, they tear fathers and breadwinners away from orphaned families and prepare them for slaughter. And the worse the position of the Russians becomes, the more unconscionably do the journalists lie, converting shameful defeats into victories, conscious that no one will contradict them, and quietly gathering in money from subscriptions and the sales of their papers. The more money and labor is spent on the war, the more do all the chiefs and contractors steal, knowing that no one will expose them since everyone is doing the same. The military, trained for murder, and having spent decades in a school of brutality, coarseness, and idleness, rejoices (poor fellows) because, besides getting an increase in pay, the casualties among their superiors create vacancies for them. Christian ministers continue to incite men to the greatest of crimes, hypocritically calling upon God to help in the work of war; and instead of condemning the pastor who, cross in hand and at the very scene of the crime, encourages men to murder, they justify and acclaim him.

The same thing goes on in Japan. The benighted Japanese fling themselves into murder with even greater ardor because of their victories, imitating all that is worst in Europe. The Mikado also holds reviews and bestows rewards. Different generals boast themselves, imagining that they have acquired Western culture by having learned to kill. Their poor unfortunate laboring people, torn from their useful work and from their families, groan as ours do. Their journalists tell lies and rejoice at an increased circulation. And probably (for where murder is acclaimed as heroism, every vice is bound to flourish) all the commanders and contractors make money. Nor do the Japanese theologians and religious teachers lag behind our European ones. As their military men are up to date in the technique of armaments, so are their theologians up to date in the technique of deception and hypocrisy – not merely tolerating but also justifying murder, which Buddha forbade.

The learned Buddhist Soyen-Shaku, who rules over eight hundred monasteries, explains that though Buddha forbade manslaughter, he also said that he could not be at peace until all beings are united in the infinitely loving heart of all things, and that to bring the discordant into harmony it is necessary to fight and kill people.[7]

---

[7] In his article it is said: "The triune world is my own possession. All things therein are my children... All are but reflections of myself. They are all from the one source... All partake of the one body. Therefore I cannot be at rest until every being, even the smallest possible fragment of existence, is settled down to its proper appointment...

"This is the position taken by the Buddha, and we, his humble followers, are but to walk in his wake.

"Why then do we fight at all?

"Because the world is not as it ought to be. Because there are here so many perverted

And it is as though the Christian and the Buddhist teachings of the oneness of the human spirit, the brotherhood of man, love, compassion, and the inviolability of human life, had never existed. Men already enlightened by the truth, both Japanese and Russian, fly at one another like wild beasts and worse than wild beasts, with the sole desire to destroy as many lives as possible. Thousands of unfortunates already groan and writhe in cruel suffering and die in agony in Japanese and Russian field hospitals, asking themselves in perplexity why this fearful thing was done to them. Other thousands are rotting in the earth or on the earth, or floating in the sea, bloated and decomposing. And tens of thousands of fathers, mothers, wives, and children weep for the breadwinners who have perished so uselessly.

But all this is not enough, and more and more fresh victims are continually being prepared. The chief concern of the Russian organizers of the slaughter is that the supply of cannon-fodder (three thousand men a day doomed to destruction) should not cease for a single day. The Japanese are similarly preoccupied. The locusts are being driven into the river incessantly, so that the later comers may pass over the bodies of the drowned...

When will it end? When will the deceived people come to themselves and say, "Well, go yourselves, you heartless and godless tsars, mikados, ministers, metropolitans, abbots, generals, editors, and contractors, or whatever you are called. Go yourselves and face the shells and bullets! We don't want to go, and won't go. Leave us in peace to plough, sow, build, and feed you, our parasites!" To say that would be so natural now in Russia, amid the weeping and wailing of hundreds of thousands of mothers, wives, and children from whom their breadwinners – the so-called reservists – are being taken. Those same reservists are, for the most part, able to read. They know what the Far East is. And they know that the war is carried on not for anything at all necessary for the Russian people, but on account of dealings in some alien "leased land" (as they call it) where it seemed advantageous to some contractors to build a railway and engage in other affairs for profit. They also know, or can know, that they will be killed like sheep in a slaughter-house, for the Japanese have the newest and most perfect instruments of murder and we have not, for the Russian authorities who are sending our people to death did not think in time of procuring such weapons as the Japanese have. Knowing all this, it would be so natural to say, "Go yourselves, you who started this affair, all of you to whom the war seems necessary and who justify it! *You* go

creatures, so many wayward thoughts, so many ill-directed hearts due to ignorant subjectivity. For this reason Buddhists are never tired of combating all the products of ignorance, and their fight must be continued to the bitter end. They will give no quarter. They will mercilessly destroy the very root from which arises the misery of this life. To accomplish this they will never be afraid of sacrificing their lives..."

The quotation continues (as such discourses do among us) with confused reflections about self-sacrifice, the absence of malice, the transmigration of souls, and much else – all merely to conceal Buddha's clear and simple command not to kill.

It is further said: "The hand that is raised to strike, and the eye that is fixed to take aim, do not belong to the individual but are the instruments utilized by the Source, which stands above our transient existence." (From *The Open Court*, May 1904. *Buddhist Views of War*, by the Right Rev. Soyen-Shaku.)

and expose yourselves to the Japanese bullets and torpedoes. We will no longer go, because it is not only unnecessary for us, but we cannot understand why it should be necessary for anyone."

But they do not say this. They go, and will go, and cannot but go, as long as they fear that which destroys the body, and not that which destroys both body and soul.

"Whether they will kill or mutilate us in some Chinnampos or whatever they are called, where we are being driven, is uncertain," they argue. "Perhaps we may get away alive, and even with rewards and glory, like those sailors who are being so feted all over Russia just now because the Japanese bombs and bullets hit someone else instead of them. But if we refuse, we shall certainly be put in prison, starved, beaten, and exiled to the province of Yakútsk, or perhaps even killed immediately." And so they go with despair in their hearts, leaving their wives and children and their rational lives.

Yesterday I met a reservist accompanied by his mother and his wife. They were all three riding in a cart. He was rather tipsy, and his wife's face was swollen with weeping. He addressed me:

"Good-bye, Lëv Nikoláevich! I'm off to the Far East."

"What! Are you going to fight?"

"Well, someone has to fight!"

"No one should fight!"

He considered. "But what can I do? Where can I escape to?"

I saw that he understood me and had understood that the affair on which he was being sent was a bad one.

"Where can I escape to?" It is the precise expression of the mental condition that is rendered in the official and journalistic world by the words: "For the Faith, the Tsar, and the Fatherland!" Those who go to suffering and death, abandoning their hungry families, say what they feel: *"Where can I escape to?"* Those who sit in safety in their luxurious palaces say that all Russians are ready to lay down their lives for their adored monarch, and for the glory and greatness of Russia.

Yesterday I received two letters, one after the other, from a peasant I know. This was the first:

DEAR LËV NIKOLÁEVICH:

Well, today I have received the official announcement summoning me to serve, and tomorrow I must present myself at the place appointed. That is all, and then to the Far East to meet Japanese bullets.

I will not tell you of my own and my family's grief, for you will not fail to understand all the horror of my position and of war. You have painfully realized that long ago and understand it all. I have all the time wished to come to see you and talk with you. I wrote you a long letter in which I described the torments of my soul, but I had not had time to make a clean copy of it when I received this summons. What is my wife to do now with our four children? Of course you, being an old man, cannot do anything for my family yourself, but you might ask some one of your friends to visit them, just for the sake of a walk. If my wife finds herself unable to bear the agony of her helplessness with all the children, and makes up her mind to go to you for help and advice, I beg you earnestly to receive her and console her. Though she does not know you personally, she believes in you, and that means a great deal.

I cannot resist the summons, but I say beforehand that not one Japanese family shall be orphaned by me. O God, how dreadful all this is! How grievous and painful it is to abandon all that one lives by and with which one is concerned.

The second letter was this:

KIND LËV NIKOLÁEVICH:

Only one day of actual service has passed, but I have already lived through an eternity of most desperate torments. From eight o'clock in the morning until nine in the evening we were crowded and pushed about in the barrack yard like a herd of cattle. The comedy of a medical examination was repeated three times, and all who reported themselves ill did not receive even ten minutes' attention before they were marked "fit." When we, two thousand fit men, were driven from the military commander's at the barracks, a crowd of relations, mothers, and wives with children in their arms, stretched out for nearly a kilometer along the road. You should have seen how they clung to their sons and husbands and fathers, and heard how desperately they wailed as they did so! Usually I behave with restraint and can control my feelings, but I could not hold out this time, and I too wept! (In journalistic language this is expressed by, "The patriotic emotion displayed was immense.") How can one measure the wholesale woe that is now spreading over almost a third of the world? And we, we are now food for cannon, which in the near future will be offered up in sacrifice to a God of revenge and horror...

I am quite unable to maintain my inner balance. Oh, how I hate myself for this double-mindedness, which prevents my serving one Lord and God...

That man does not yet believe sufficiently that what destroys the body is not terrible, but that is terrible which destroys both body and soul. And so he cannot refuse the service. But yet, while leaving his family he promises in advance that not one Japanese family shall be orphaned through him. He believes in the chief law of God, the law of all religions: to do to others as you wish them to do to you. And in our time there are not thousands but millions of men who more or less consciously recognize that law – not Christians only, but Buddhists, Muslims, Confucians, and Brahmins as well.

True heroes really exist – not those who are now feted because, having wished to kill others, they themselves escaped – but true heroes who are now confined in prisons and in the province of Yakútsk for having categorically refused to enter the ranks of the murderers, and have preferred martyrdom to the renunciation of the law of Christ. There are also men like the one who wrote to me, and who will go but will not kill. And even the majority who go without thinking, or trying not to think, of what they are doing, feel in the depths of their souls that they are doing wrong to obey the authorities, who tear men from their work and their families and send them needlessly to slaughter – a thing repugnant to their souls and to their faith. They only go because they are so entangled on all sides that they exclaim, *"Where can I escape to?"*

And those who remain at home not only feel but also know this, and express it. Yesterday on the high road I met some peasants returning from Túla. One of them, walking beside his empty cart, was reading a leaflet.

"What is that?" I asked. "A telegram?"

He stopped. "This is yesterday's, but I have today's as well."

He took another out of his pocket. We stopped and I read it.

"You should have seen what it was like at the station yesterday," he said. "It was terrible. Wives and children, more than a thousand of them, were all crying and sobbing. They surrounded the train but could not board it. Even strangers looking on were in tears. One Túla woman cried out and died on the spot. She had five children. The children were shoved into different asylums, but the father was sent on all the same… And what do we want with this Manchuria, or whatever it is called? We have much land of our own. And what a lot of people have been killed and what a lot of money wasted…"

Yes, the people's attitude to war is quite different now from what it used to be, even in '77.[8] People never reacted then as they do now.

The papers write that at receptions of the Tsar (who is travelling about Russia to hypnotize the people who are being sent off to slaughter) indescribable enthusiasm is shown among the populace. In reality, something quite different is happening. One hears on all sides reports of how in one place three reservists hung themselves, and in another two more. One hears how a woman whose husband had been taken brought her three children to the recruiting office and left them there, while another woman hanged herself in the yard of the military commander's home. Everyone is dissatisfied, gloomy, and embittered. People no longer react to the words, "For the Faith, the Tsar, and the Fatherland!" the national anthem, and shouts of "Hurrah!" as they used to do. A war of a different kind, a struggling consciousness of the wrongfulness and sin of the thing to which men are being called, is taking place.

---

[8] The Russo-Turkish War of 1877-8.–A.M.

Yes, the great strife of our time is not that now taking place between the Japanese and the Russians, nor that which may blaze up between the White and the Yellow races. It is not the strife carried on by torpedoes, bullets, and bombs, but that spiritual strife which has unceasingly gone on, and is now going on, between the enlightened consciousness of mankind, which is now awaiting its manifestation, and the darkness and oppression which surrounds and burdens mankind.

Christ yearned in expectation in his own time, and said, "I came to cast fire upon the earth, and how I wish that it were already kindled." (Luke 12:49) What Christ longed for is being accomplished. The fire is kindling. Let us not check it, but promote it.

April 30th, 1904

CHAPTER XIII

I should never finish this article if I continued to add to it all that confirms its chief thought. Yesterday news was received of the sinking of Japanese battleships. In what are called the higher circles of Russian fashionable society, wealthy and intelligent people are rejoicing, with no prickings of conscience, at the destruction of thousands of human lives. And today I have received from a simple seaman, a man of the lowest rank of society, the following letter:[9]

Much respected Lëv Nikoláevich:

I greet you with a low bow and with love, much respected Lëv Nikoláevich. I have read your book. It was very pleasant reading for me. I am very fond of reading what you write, and as we are now in military action. Lëv Nikoláevich, will you please tell me whether or not it is pleasing to God that our commanders compel us to kill. I beg you to write me, Lëv Nikoláevich, please, whether or not truth exists now on earth. At the church service the priest speaks of the Christ-loving army. Is it true or not that God loves war? Please, Lëv Nikoláevich, have you any books showing whether truth exists on earth or not? Send me such books and I will pay what they cost. I beg you not to neglect my request, Lëv Nikoláevich. If there are no such books, then write to me. I shall be very glad to receive a letter from you and shall await it with impatience.

Now farewell. I remain alive and well and wish you the same from the Lord God. Good health and good success in your work.

[Then follows the address, Port Arthur, the name of his ship, his rank, and his Christian name, patronymic, and family name.]

I cannot reply directly to that good, serious, and truly enlightened man. He is in Port Arthur, with which there is no longer any communication either by post or by telegraph. But we still have a means of mutual communication: God, in whom we both believe and concerning whom we both know that military "action" displeases him. The doubt that has arisen in the man's soul is at the same time its own solution. And that doubt has now arisen and lives in the souls of thousands and thousands of men, not Russians and Japanese only, but all those unfortunate people who are forcibly compelled to do things most repugnant to human nature.

---

[9] This letter in the Russian is ungrammatical, badly spelled, badly punctuated, and with capital letters constantly misused.–A.M.

The hypnotism by which the rulers have stupefied and still try to stupefy people soon passes off and its effect grows ever weaker and weaker; whereas the doubt *"whether or not it is pleasing to God that our commanders compel us to kill"* grows stronger and stronger. It can in no way be extinguished and is spreading more and more widely.

The doubt *"whether or not it is pleasing to God that our commanders compel us to kill"* is that spark which Christ brought down upon earth, and which begins to kindle.

And to know and feel this is a great joy.

Yásnaya Polyána, May 8, 1904

Lector House believes that a society develops through a two-fold approach of continuous learning and adaptation, which is derived from the study of classic literary works spread across the historic timeline of literature records. Therefore, we aim at reviving, repairing and redeveloping all those inaccessible or damaged but historically as well as culturally important literature across subjects so that the future generations may have an opportunity to study and learn from past works to embark upon a journey of creating a better future.

This book is a result of an effort made by Lector House towards making a contribution to the preservation and repair of original ancient works which might hold historical significance to the approach of continuous learning across subjects.

HAPPY READING & LEARNING!

LECTOR HOUSE LLP
E-MAIL: lectorpublishing@gmail.com

www.ingramcontent.com/pod-product-compliance
Lightning Source LLC
Chambersburg PA
CBHW021356160726
47994CB00007B/2976